Michael Billett was born in Dorchester and has lived in various parts of Dorset for many years. He now resides in Poole with his wife, Helen. They have two daughters, Sonia and Jennifer. He is the author of several books on countryside matters, including *Thatching and Thatched Buildings*, *Thatched Buildings of Dorset* and *A History of English Country Sports*. Michael Billett is also the author of *Highwaymen and Outlaws* and several technical books relating to the oil industry. He is a Bachelor of Science and a Doctor of Philosophy.

Following page
Hammoon Manor House, with parts dating to the sixteenth century. The L-shaped building served as the farmhouse to nearby Manor Farm. Few buildings of such a size have remained thatched since first being built.

DISCOVER DORSET

FARMHOUSES AND COTTAGES

MICHAEL BILLETT

THE DOVECOTE PRESS

Scoles Farm, built with Purbeck stone rubble in the seventeenth century, incorporates what was once a small independent medieval hall house.

First published in 2002 by The Dovecote Press Ltd
Stanbridge, Wimborne, Dorset BH21 4JD

ISBN 1 874336 78 4

Series designed by Humphrey Stone

Typeset in Monotype Sabon
Printed and bound by Baskerville Press, Salisbury, Wiltshire

A CIP catalogue record for this book is available from the British Library

1 3 5 7 9 8 6 4 2

CONTENTS

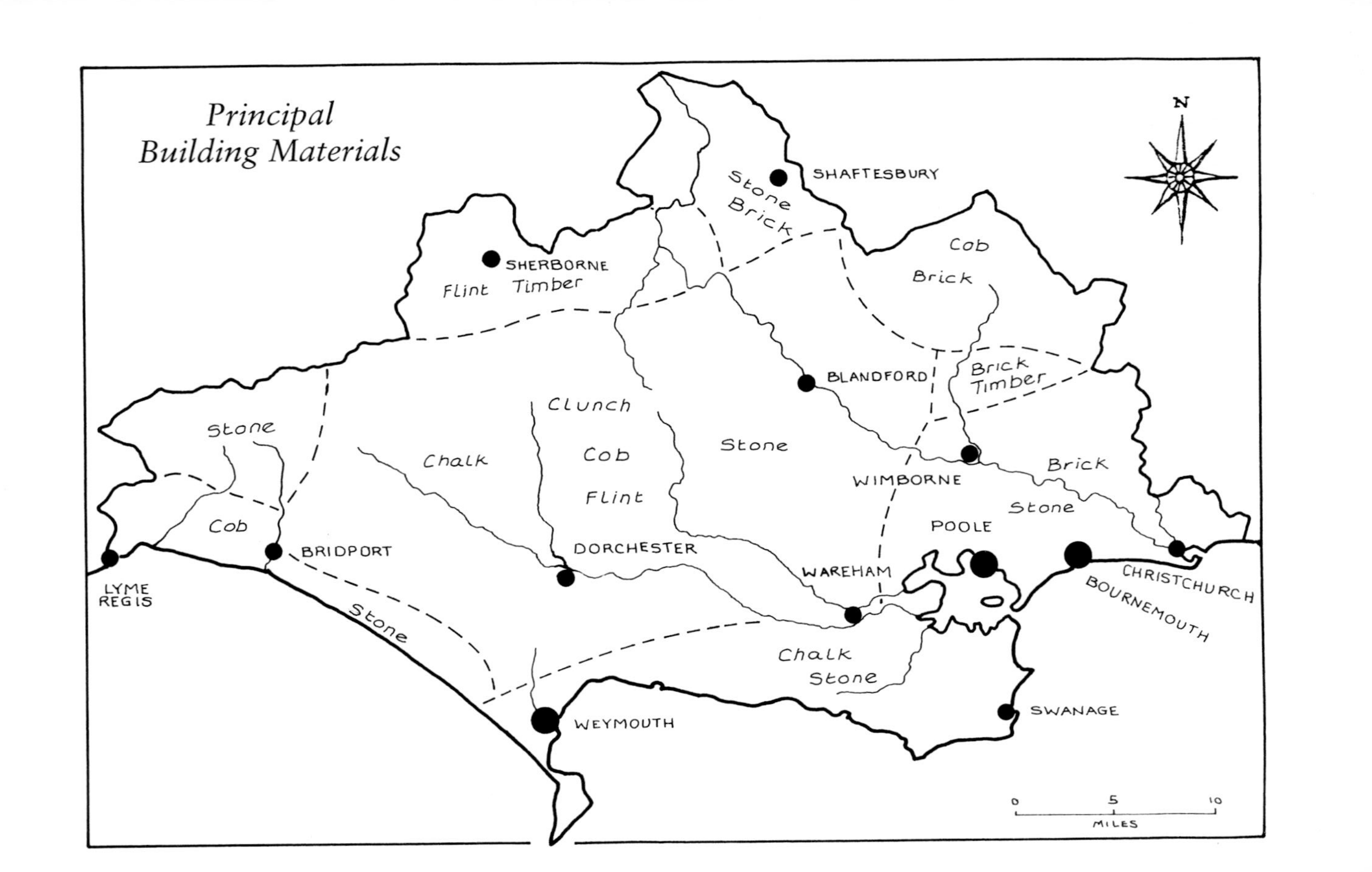
Principal
Building Materials
N
SHAFTESBURY
Stone
Brick
SHERBORNE
Flint
Timber
Cob
Brick
BLANDFORD
Brick
Timber
Clunch
Cob
Flint
Stone
Stone
Chalk
WIMBORNE
Brick
Stone
POOLE
Cob
BRIDPORT
DORCHESTER
WAREHAM
LYME REGIS
CHRISTCHURCH
BOURNEMOUTH
Stone
Chalk
Stone
WEYMOUTH
SWANAGE
0
5
10
MILES

BUILDING MATERIALS

Over the course of millions of years, nature laid down geological formations in Dorset that have yielded a rich variety of potentially useful building materials. Before the eighteenth century, cottages were usually built with those that were most readily available. For example, soft fine-particle chalk dug from the downs was widely used for the wall construction of cottages and barns.

In the south-west and north-east of the county, the chalk was mainly used in the form of cob, a mixture of powdered chalk and clay, with the addition of chopped straw as a binder. Usually, at least three parts of chalk were incorporated for each part of clay. The lack of structural strength of cob limited its use to one-storey and very occasionally two-storey cottages. Higher proportions of chalk produced a stronger wall. In the sixteenth and seventeenth centuries, the cob was trampled, without using shuttering, and the wall height gradually increased, as each layer dried and hardened. This gave the final wall a delightful uneven appearance and it was often two to three feet thick. Excessive damp weakened cob walls, so they were constructed on stone, or later brick, foundations. The overhang of the eaves of a thatched roof shielded the top of the wall from falling rain. This dual protection gave rise to the expression, 'all cob wants is a hat and a pair of shoes'. The chalk hills sweep south-westwards from Cranborne Chase through Blandford and Milton Abbas to Beaminster. A smaller outcrop turns south-east at Portesham, running through Dorchester and West Lulworth before continuing on to form the Purbeck hills.

Large blocks of pure chalk, known as clunch or chalk ashlar, were occasionally cut for building purposes, as it was easy to quarry and

Map showing the wide range of locally available materials used for wall construction in vernacular buildings.

A seventeenth-century chalk ashlar and cob cottage at Higher Kingcombe, with a modern slate roof porch addition. Parts of the cottage formerly served as a dairy.

Ower Farmhouse, the building to the right with a central chimney stack was constructed in the late seventeenth or early eighteenth century. The extension to the left, with gabled attics, was added in the nineteenth century; alternating bands of rust-brown 'pudding stones' were used for its wall construction.

A seventeenth-century stone-built cottage at Brandy Row, Portland, as it looked in 1899. It was one of the last of many such types that were common on the island. Thatch was still in use, as local stone was not easily cleaved for roofing slates, as was Purbeck stone.

dress. In addition, chalk rubble was often used to construct the walls of more humble cottages. The chalk also yielded considerable quantities of flints, a hard variety of quartz. These were much used for rubble-walling, especially in the area around Dorchester. From the beginning of the seventeenth century, flints were frequently used for better class cottages, in admixture with chalk, stones and later bricks; often in the form of decorative alternating bands. Such mixtures produced very attractive and durable walls. In north Dorset, less elaborate cottages were sometimes built entirely from stones called 'pudding stones', picked up at random from the fields.

Dorset was additionally fortunate in possessing several outcrops of hard limestones, as well as the softer chalks. These yielded good building stones for wall and roofing slates. At various times, the harder limestones were quarried at Portland, Purbeck, Marnhull, Sturminster Newton, Portesham and Poxwell. Masons dressed and carved the stones into blocks suitable for building. Portland's now famous oolitic limestone is a prime example of a hard-wearing material that can be very precisely carved. Although quarried from Norman times, Portland stone was expensive to work and except on Portland itself was not greatly favoured for house building in Dorset

A thatched farmhouse at Studland in the 1940s. It shows the dual use of thatch and Purbeck stone slates on adjacent buildings. This area was once the village centre, but the farmhouse has since been demolished.

until the eighteenth century. This was well after its virtues had been highlighted by the designs of Inigo Jones and later Sir Christopher Wren for prestige buildings in London.

In the Swanage area, Purbeck stone was mined from underground tunnels, called galleries, but later it was extracted from open-cast quarries. The stone is a good material for wall construction and many cottages and farm buildings were built with it, especially between Swanage and Dorchester. The laminated nature of the stone also allowed it to be easily cleaved into roofing slates, although it was not a true slate. The stones' heavy weight demanded a strong timber framework to support the load; in contrast, for example, to the lighter rafters needed to support thatch. In many cases, the immense weight of the slates restricted their use to a few courses above the eaves level, the remainder of the roof being covered with tiles. This was particularly prevalent in the Wareham area.

An unusual shell limestone, called Purbeck Marble was also

quarried; the shells present within the stone having originated from the fossilized remains of freshwater pond snails. Although not a true marble, polishing produced a high sheen; from the thirteenth and fourteenth centuries this property was exploited widely for church decoration. A few old cottages in Purbeck still have small blocks of Purbeck marble, engraved in geometrical designs, over their doorways. In the north-west, an imported limestone from Ham Hill in Somerset beautified many cottage walls: after it weathered the golden-brown surface attracted lichens, which enhanced the characteristic mellow warm nature of the stone.

Despite the presence of London clay type deposits in parts of Dorset, brick making was unusual until the seventeenth century. At first, brick houses were generally restricted to the more sandy regions of the county. The use of brick increased in the eighteenth century, becoming especially common in the Poole area. Small-scale brick making later spread further afield, whilst the growing population in

A seventeenth century cob and thatched cottage at Church Knowle. The walls were later refaced with bricks, after they became more readily available in the late seventeenth and early eighteenth centuries. The brick built extension to the right was added in early Victorian times.

The remains of a mid nineteenth-century brick kiln on Powerstock Common. The nearby disused railway that ran parallel to the Common allowed transportation of its production.

Victorian times increased demand for better quality cottages – the eventual catalyst for the construction of several large-scale brickworks. The one at Gillingham, opened in 1865, produced bright red bricks that were widely used in north Dorset, and are still familiar today. Several brickworks developed at Broadmayne, manufacturing the characteristic brown brick speckled with black, common around Dorchester: traces of manganese oxide in the clay produced the speckled effect during firing. In the west of the county, a Suffolk-type brick kiln was constructed on Powerstock Common in 1857. Throughout the county, the coming of the railways in the nineteenth century further accelerated the use of brick for building.

Oak grew well in the London clay in the east of the county. Despite this, little timber-framed or cruck house building took place. Any surviving medieval timber-framing exists in one of two basic forms, cruck or post-and-truss construction, and is most common at Holt, Sturminster Marshall, Cerne Abbas and in a few wooded areas in the north of the county, near Sherborne. Sturminster Newton contains a good selection of houses built with a wide variety of materials, including Tudor-type timbering, red brick, cob, stone, and thatch.

With regard to roofing materials, tile manufacture in Dorset took place on a small scale from the seventeenth century, but was mainly confined to the south-east of the county. Once the railway reached Dorset and Welsh slates became available in cheap commercial quantities, imported slate competed with the traditional thatch for cottage and farmhouse construction.

The main type of thatching material used in Dorset was straw, obtained from the wheat sown on the chalk downland. The two main forms were long straw, used mainly in the east of the county and the more widely utilized combed wheat reed. The long straw roof gave rise to a more random and natural looser appearance on the roof

An example of a thatched timber-framed building with brick in-filling at Higher Dairy Cottage, Cowgrove.

A thatcher at work at West Borough, Wimborne, in 1914.
Plain roof ridges were then favoured rather than the raised decorated block ridges now in fashion. The cottage on the left is still thatched today.

than the more bristly appearance of combed wheat reed. The latter type of material was obtained by first removing the grain from the wheat ears and then arranging the stalks in a parallel form, lying in one direction, with the thicker butt ends of the straw together on the roof.

In a handful of isolated pockets, reed was used instead of straw. Reed beds were once cultivated in the marshes at the back of the Fleet near Abbotsbury Swannery, but the supply is now limited and reserved for specialized local use. Reed was also grown at Radipole Lake and at Lodmoor, but these marsh reed beds, like Abbotsbury, have drastically declined. Heather was also used for thatching, especially where it was most readily available on the heathland in the east of the county. The construction of thatched roofs also required a

Cutting reed by hand for thatching at Abbotsbury in the 1930's. Hand cut reeds possess better mechanical stability than modern machine cut ones.

good supply of thatching spars to fix the thatch securely to the roof. Traditionally, local hurdle-makers supplied spars cut from hazel, but although coppicing continues on a small scale the number of hurdle-makers still at work in the county has fallen dramatically over the years.

The same is true with thatching material. It is now estimated that over seventy percent of the reed thatch used in this country comes from eastern Europe; from Austria, Hungary, Turkey, Poland and Romania. At least one Dorset thatcher imports veldt grass from South Africa as an alternative to combed wheat reed, which is in short supply. There is also a shortage of long straw, as the special wheat varieties are no longer grown. The continued intrusion of imported materials, in place of local materials, will in time change the traditional appearance of many of Dorset's villages. English Heritage have suggested that the re-thatching of a listed building should be made a planning matter. The majority of thatchers in Dorset try to adhere to traditional materials and style, but some insist on the freedom to put the best material they can obtain on their clients' roofs.

FARMHOUSES

Until recently, much of the agricultural land in Dorset was owned by a handful of families, and the majority of farmers were their tenants. Sheep dominated Dorset farming until the early eighteenth century and the present enclosed downland farms, now growing wheat, were previously open fields grazed by immense flocks. The west of the county has generally been devoted to dairy farming, together with the Blackmore Vale in the north. Thomas Hardy's concept of the 'Vale of the Little Dairies' still holds good today, except that the dairies in the Blackmore Vale are now generally larger. Although some smallholdings existed, the majority who worked on the land were recruited by the farmers at hiring fairs, who drew on a stock of often poverty-stricken landless labourers. As the number of paupers increased in the seventeenth and eighteenth centuries, individual parishes administered a form of poor relief, some even building parish poor houses and cottages.

Most of Dorset's older farmhouses have undergone endless modifications since they were first built, both to adapt to new farming techniques and the improving lifestyles of the farmers and their families. In the nineteenth century, many smaller farms amalgamated to form larger units and today the total number of farms in Dorset stands at just under 3,000. Most of the older farmhouses surviving in Dorset are vernacular buildings built with local materials and roofed with thatch or stone slates. A good example is Scotland Farm, north of Corfe Castle. The stone farmhouse was built one storey high with attics, and its walls were probably recycled from the rubble of the ruined medieval castle after its demolition during the Civil War. The roof was covered with stone slates.

Older farmhouses often formed part of the farmyard. Only during the later Georgian period were the larger farmhouses built a short distance away from their ancillary buildings, such as barns and

Scotland Farm in Purbeck, near New Mills Heath. Built in 1665 by WilliamWhefer with an attractive stone porch as a central doorway.

milking parlours. The improving social status of the farmer demanded that he live separately from his livestock and labourers. Previously, master and labourers often ate together at the same table. There existed a large variation in the relative sizes of farmhouses, ranging from the simple small two-roomed cottage, originally built on smallholdings, to the larger farmhouses of the prosperous yeoman farmer.

The few old farmsteads still located in Dorset villages are usually the survivors from the period of communal open-field agriculture, roughly from the later medieval period right through to the mid-eighteenth century. The newer more isolated farmsteads can often be dated to the Parliamentary Enclosure of the surrounding common land, which in turn allowed the establishment of a new central farmstead. Dorset clung on to the open-field system of agriculture for much longer than many parts of England, and although a handful of strip fields still remain on Portland today, most of Dorset's open fields had been enclosed by 1876: the year that saw the dramatic enclosure of the 3,500 acres of Fordington's open fields around Dorchester.

Eventually, redundant farmhouses in the villages were converted into two or more cottages for farm workers. Many of the old barns in

Cottages at Iwerne Stepleton. Before conversion, they were the hunt kennels of Peter Beckford, the eighteenth-century fox-hunting enthusiast.

villages suffered a similar treatment. Even the eighteenth-century hunt kennels at Iwerne Stepleton were transformed into cottages. The kennels formerly housed the foxhounds of Peter Beckford, who hunted over Cranborne Chase and who in 1781 published *Thoughts on Hunting,* the classic book on fox-hunting. However, not all farmers moved house, and a scattering of villages throughout the county still retain a working farm at their heart.

From the early Middle Ages to the middle of the eighteenth century, farmhouses were nearly always built one room deep. This meant that to incorporate several rooms, the building had to be long, rather than square. The narrow depth of the long-house encouraged the use of thatch as a cheap roof covering, as it was easy to achieve a steep roof pitch to shed rainwater. The earliest medieval long-houses had the dwelling-house and cow-byre in a single range. Although the doorways were usually about three feet wide, a few were considerably wider, usually to allow long-horned cattle to enter. In the seventeenth century, the original long-houses were often adapted by building wings at right angles to the older part, giving rise to cross-wing farmhouses, which in Dorset were again often thatched.

The long-house design invariably included a through-passage that divided the living quarters from the various service rooms. Later, in a

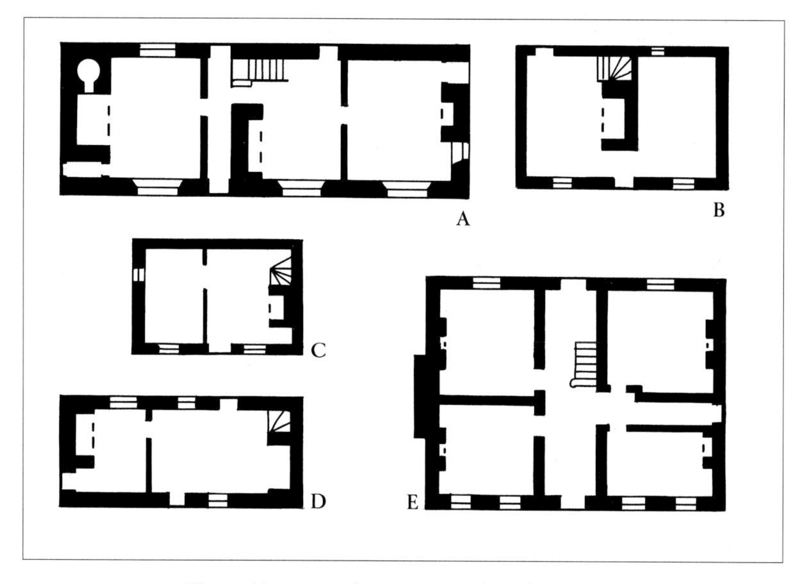

Plan of house styles associated with Dorset.
A – Cross-passage with three heated rooms. B – Lobby entry, one heated room and one unheated. C – Gable end stack, again one room heated and one unheated. D – Gable end stack with two heated rooms.
E – Double pile consisting of four rooms with three heated.

large farmhouse and manor house a hall became a status symbol and formed an advancement on the more primitive long-house. The basic plan was a ground-floor hall open to the roof between a two-storey solar wing and a service end. The solar living quarters included a parlour or private room. A hall built on the first floor later came into fashion, keeping the ground floor exclusively for general storage.

An early example of a hall house may be found at Barnston Farm, the former manor house at Church Knowle (for illustration see following page). The farmhouse was built at the end of the thirteenth century, with stone walls, under a stone-slated roof. In this case, the solar wing was built in the centre of the farmhouse, dividing the ground-floor hall from the west wing. Alterations were made to the house in the sixteenth century to improve the amount of light entering the solar wing and an extra floor was inserted in the hall to provide extra accommodation.

The thirteenth-century Barnston Farm, Church Knowle, was altered in the sixteenth century by dividing the hall and inserting an extra floor.

Another example is found at Naish Farm, at Holwell, near Sherborne. This medieval farmhouse has a hall between the two-storey solar end and the now partly altered one-storey service end, on the other side of the through-passage. When the farmhouse was first built with stone rubble walling in the fifteenth century, the single-storey hall was open to the underside of the thatch roof, but a century later the hall was chambered over to provide extra rooms upstairs.

In the seventeenth and eighteenth centuries, service rooms became an integral part of the farmhouse, and were no longer divided from the main living quarters by a through-passage. The entrance to the house

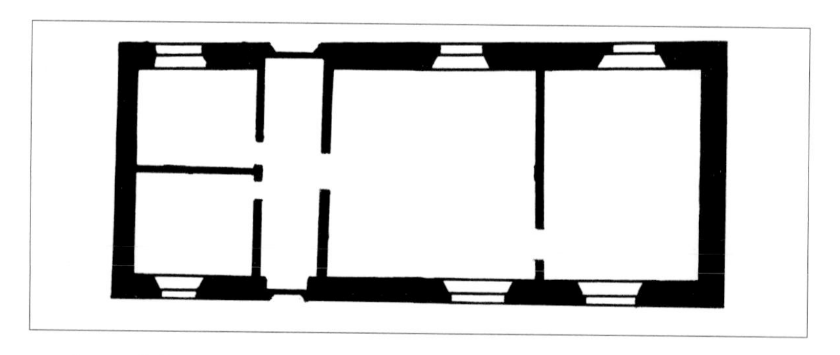

Ground floor plan, showing use of through passage to separate solar rooms from service end at Naish Farm, Holwell.

In the eighteenth century, George Boswell, a pioneer of irrigation, resided at Waddock Farm, Affpuddle, and designed the nearby water meadows.

was gained either through a lobby, or by a direct-entry door. Many examples of such properties abound in Dorset. One may be found at Waddock Cross, just north of Affpuddle. The large two-storey house, called Waddock Farm, was built with red brick under a thatched roof, in the early eighteenth century, for use as a dairy and farmhouse. Three wings branched out from the main block and a central doorway gave direct-entry to the house. The front of the building faced north but it was 'turned about' in 1797 to provide a southerly aspect. The alterations to the façade gave the farmhouse a formal back and an informal front. A porch entrance was added at the same time.

In the Georgian period, towards the end of the eighteenth century, the double-pile manor farmhouse, two rooms deep, became established in Dorset. These larger farmhouses, reflecting the increased prosperity and social aspirations of many farmers, were much squarer in design. Their geometric shape enabled them to be roofed with slates or tiles, rather than thatch; the roof pitch angle was reduced. The simplest version of the double-pile farmhouse consisted of four rooms downstairs; a living-room and a sitting-room in the front and a kitchen and another service room, such as a pantry or dairy at the back. A staircase at the rear rose between the service rooms to the upper floor. The front door was constructed in the centre of the main elevation. All principal rooms possessed a fireplace, built

Watermeadow House, Hooke. An imposing modern farmhouse attractively set on the edge of the village, surrounded by its dairy farmland.

in the end gable walls. A good example is North Holton Farm at Lytchett Minster, built with brick under a tiled roof. Larger versions of the double-pile farmhouse were built with sideways extensions, thereby retaining the basic design principal of two rooms deep.

Two of the earliest double-pile farmhouses constructed in Dorset were Manor Farm, Dewlish, and Manor Farm, Wynford Eagle. Both were built in the early seventeenth century, well over a century before the design became widespread in Dorset. The Manor Farm at Dewlish was built with banded flint and stone, under a slate roof, with a central doorway. In the case of Manor Farm at Wynford Eagle, a stone eagle still perches on the top gable of the central porch, with a stone dated 1630. Again some walls are of banded flint and stone, whilst others are stone rubble faced with ashlar; the roof is tiled.

The majority of the older farmhouses, with the exception of some of the larger manor farmhouses, rarely saw the hand of an architect. Most were built using well-established practical building traditions, employing simple techniques and economical use of materials. The use of brick for farmhouses in Dorset became common during the eighteenth and nineteenth centuries and this trend dominated the twentieth century. As farmers became wealthier, they employed professional surveyors and architects to design their houses. A good example of an imposing late twentieth-century farmhouse, Watermeadow House, may be found at Hooke, It lies on the opposite side of the road to a typical Victorian farmhouse, Bridge Farm.

COTTAGES

In the past, Dorset country cottages presented a far from ideal picture. Most were miserable hovels that sheltered the labourer, his wife, several children and often a grandparent and lodger. The gloomy and unhealthy damp interior offered at the most two rooms, both to live and sleep in. In some better-built cottages a bread oven was built into the wall beside the fireplace. Water was drawn from a well, as there was no running water or sanitation. There were, of course, exceptions. For example, in the Regency period, the wealthy built themselves

Former rope workers cottages in Mill Street, Burton Bradstock. The upper windows placed below the eaves level avoid interrupting the roof line and the need for 'eyebrow' windows cut into the thatch.

Terraced cottages at Wakeham, Portland, with characteristic gabled porches and slate roofs to provide protection against the weather.

beautifully designed ornamented cottages in the fashionable cottage *ornée* style. Prosperous landowners also occasionally planned so-called model cottages for their estate workers.

In the 1830's the situation worsened. The invention of the threshing machine made many labourers redundant, leading to cottages being abandoned. In 1843, a government commission drew attention to the appalling living conditions endured by the rural poor in Dorset, many of whom were living in unheated temporary hovels. In the decade following 1846, after the Corn Laws were repealed, a few farmers started to build tied cottages for their workers, in rows of four or six. The enclosure movement in Dorset was so gradual it had little effect on cottage building; in fact more were destroyed than built. In 1876, the average number of people living in each cottage was still seven.

For the vast majority, living conditions only started to improve towards the end of the nineteenth century, when employers found it essential to retain labour. As well as cottages for farm labourers, some were built to house workers in the rope industry at Bridport and Burton Bradstock (see page 23), for weavers at Stoke Abbott, for stone masons on Portland and Purbeck and for those involved in the ball clay industry. The terraced cottages at Wakeham, Portland, traditionally incorporated stone porches to protect their doors from the weather. In the early days of radio, a few cottages were constructed for wireless workers, near Dorchester. Railway workers also sometimes lived in their employer's rented cottages, as did some brewery employees.

The materials used for cottage construction varied across the county, depending on what was cheapest and most locally available, saving transport costs. Different cottage styles therefore evolved. In the northern vales, in the Sherborne region, limestone from the local quarries was much used for cottage building, as was some imported limestone from Ham Hill. Along the southern coastal region from Portland to Swanage, stone rubble was favoured, as it was in the Blackmore and Marshwood Vales, where little timber had been available since the sixteenth century. In some western and north-east regions, cob and flint were preferred, but in the chalkland parishes of Winterborne St Martin and Steepleton limestone from the Upwey quarry was mixed with flint. The Piddletrenthide area produced the attractive walling made of flint layers alternating with chalk, or brick, in decorative bands. In the east of the county, brick and a little timber-frame building took place.

Timber was in short supply in all areas after the seventeenth century and any timber-framed buildings were by necessity kept in good repair. The in-filling consisted either of stone rubble from the scattered quarries, or brick. Brick predominated at Wareham, Bere Regis and Morden. When a village was in easy reach of both brick kilns and quarries, builders constructed some cottages in brick and others in stone, such as those seen in the main street of Stoborough. The few medieval and Tudor cottages still standing in Dorset obviously belonged to the more prosperous, as they were substantially built. Their survival owes much to chance – for fire, demolition and redevelopment have robbed the county of all but a handful.

Due to the dangers of the sea and the need to prevent smuggling, Dorset's coast is well-endowed with coastguard stations and the

Coastguard cottages on Brownsea Island, Poole Harbour, situated on the quayside and complete with Victorian crenellations.

attendant cottages. The most unusual are on Brownsea Island in Poole Harbour; where the early-nineteenth century rendered brick cottages possess castellations or battlements, including arrow slits. They also display armorial shields and the end walls are gabled with crow steps. The position of the coastguard station, near the cottages, was chosen because it faced the Harbour entrance, making it easier to control the smuggling once rife in the area.

More conventional coastguard stations were built, or sometimes rented from their owners, after the HM Coastguard Service was formed officially in January 1822. In 1856, the Admiralty took control of the Service. The two or three bedroom coastguard cottages were constructed mainly with stone in small terraces, with slate roofs. The coastguard station at Worth Matravers was constructed in a range of four in 1834. The coastguard cottages at White Nothe, overlooking Ringstead Bay were erected a little earlier; they are worthy of note because they were constructed on the 495 foot high cliff-top and constituted the highest inhabited building on the Dorset coast.

Coastguard cottages at Aldhelm's Head, Worth Matravers, originally built in a range of four cottages in 1834.

Lulworth was once a major smuggling centre and coastguard cottages bordered the lane leading down to the Cove. In the west of the county at Seatown, the cottages above the Anchor Inn were originally the coastguard station. Other prominent ones were those at Kimmeridge, Swanage and Portland, but many have now undergone development, or are let as holiday homes.

From medieval times, the church and other charitable benefactors contributed to the construction of almshouses for the needy and the old. Many Dorset almshouses trace their origins back to those early days; the Christian charitable upbringing of the wealthier Victorians added impetus to the process in the nineteenth century. Almshouses were constructed in various architectural forms. Usually, the individual rooms for the inmates were linked together in a single long one-storey row, or around a courtyard in an arcade. They shared a communal chapel and dining hall. Many almshouses possessed mullioned windows and tall chimneys, unusual for such relatively humble buildings. Inscriptions on a central outside wall shield often displayed details of their particular foundation.

Most of Dorset's almshouses are in the towns, and therefore outside the scope of this book. But those in the villages are often

Top The almshouses at Pamphill Green founded by Roger Gillingham in 1698. They stretch long and low each side of the central school house, and the eight doors indicate the number of almshouses.

Above Almshouses at Wimborne St Giles, the gift of Sir Anthony Ashley, with a fine armorial panel set above the arcade.

architecturally little different to the cottages that surround them. The almshouse at Wimborne St Giles was built around 1624 for ten residents and is attached to the church overlooking the village green. The row was constructed with red brick and stone dressings to create a single-storey building but with a two-storey centre block incorporating a three bay arcade, originally housing a common room. Later in the century, in 1674, an almshouse was founded in the old town of Milton Abbas, but after the demolition ordered by Joseph

A long stretch of thatch at Manswood, More Crichel. In addition to the 11 cottages, the roof also covers the former post office and general store.

Damer, the almshouse was re-erected in the new village in 1779. It was built with banded brick and flint, with stone dressings; the roof was tiled with verges of stone-slates.

The almshouse at Pamphill Green was constructed with William and Mary brickwork and The National Trust now owns it. A tablet records the founder; 'the pious and charitable gift of Roger Gillingham, in 1698, to God and ye Poor'. The wife of the rector, Mary Turner, founded an almshouse in Trent in 1846. It was built with rubble walls under a tiled roof; the Tudor style building contained four dwellings arranged on opposite sides of a small central courtyard. Another Victorian almshouse, called 'The Home', was erected by the Sheridan family at Frampton. The stone-built terrace has a series of porches and a biblical quotation inscribed on the end facing the church.

Any list of unusual Dorset cottages must include the terrace called 'The Buildings', at Manswood, More Crichel, which claims the longest continuous stretch of thatch in England. It extends 120 yards and envelops 11 cottages. The terrace was constructed in the eighteenth century with cob walls, but a low brick extension with a slate roof has since been added along the length of the building at the rear. Individual tiled porches shield the front doors and a series of open gaps, along the terrace, gives access to the front from the rear. In

Above The Smiths Arms, Godmanstone. The one-storeyed thatched inn measures just twelve feet in width. It was converted from a blacksmith's cottage into an inn by a Royal Charter of Charles II.

Opposite page top Umbrella Cottage at Lyme Regis may have been a former lodge or toll house.

Opposite page bottom Gaunts Lodge, Stanbridge, is an early example of an extravagantly thatched cottage *ornée*.

contrast, the former tiny thatched cottage home of a blacksmith at Godmanstone in the seventeenth century was later converted into a pub, The Smiths Arms, one of the smallest in England. The walls were constructed with cob and faced with local flint; the roof eaves measure just four feet above the ground.

An unusual cottage of a different type stands in Sidmouth Road, Lyme Regis. 'Umbrella Cottage' combines details from several periods. A huge rounded thatched roof sweeps down, umbrella-like, into cusped eaves and onto free-standing timber posts; the two front pillars display carved owls on the capitals. A central chimney protrudes through the roof. The polygonal-shaped cottage has traceried windows and boasts a carved Flemish door, probably from the sixteenth century. The flamboyant appearance of the cottage suggests it was built, or underwent extensive alterations, in the first quarter of the nineteenth century, in the cottage *ornée* style.

Goathill Lodge, near Sherborne, was probably built in the mid-nineteenth century to form an eastern entrance into Sherborne Park.

The architect John Nash was mainly responsible for the cottage *ornée* in England, which was at its most fashionable during the Regency period, 1810 to 1820. The cottages were built in an extravagant design to create an idealized image of a traditional country cottage in a romantic and picturesque form. Dorset possesses many examples, all individually designed and invariably thatched, with wide eaves. Most are fairly small and possess leaded lights windows. Thatched verandahs often surround the cottages and thatched porches usually shelter the doors.

A good example of a cottage *ornée* lodge may be found at Stanbridge, near Wimborne. It was built in about 1810, at the entrance to the drive of Gaunt's House (see previous page). The walls are constructed of brick with some infilling, forming an unusual pattern of three equal sides of a polygon, with a longer fourth side. The building has one storey but possesses a spacious attic. In keeping with its picturesque appearance, the lodge has pointed, diamond-shaped leaded-light windows, under stone lintels. A long straw thatch roof covers the building and the bottom edge of the thatch finishes with a series of cusps, to give a bold ornamental effect. The doorways

Old Came Rectory near Dorchester, the former home of William Barnes. It is a good example of a period cottage *ornée* house.

have individual thatched porches with cusped eaves and are supported on rustic timber posts.

Another lodge in a similar style stands by the roadside about a quarter-of-a-mile south of Sherborne Castle, at Goathill. The lodge was probably erected a little later than the one at Stanbridge. A massive thatch covers the lodge and wide undulating eaves protect the mellow yellow-tinged walls from rain. Three tall chimneys rise through the centre of the towering thatch.

Other cottage *ornée* lodges may be found on the Drax Estate at Morden and at Compton House, near Sherborne. The former lodge called 'The Round House' is in fact polygonal, although the roof is round. The lodge at Compton House was renovated in 1968 but still possesses an original interior ceiling, with similar bossing and carving as found in the nearby church at Nether Compton.

A true cottage *ornée*, much larger than the lodges, was once the home of rector and Dorset dialect poet, William Barnes. The rectory is situated at Winterborne Came, beside the A352 road to Broadmayne from Dorchester. The two-storey house was built with stone rubble in the early nineteenth century. As well as the tall main

The village looking east at Milton Abbas. The twenty square cottages, nearly all identical, were built in pairs on each side of the street at the behest of the autocratic landowner when he demolished the old village.

thatched roof, there are three separate thatched verandahs at the front of the house, with timber supporting posts. In addition to the small diamond and hexagonal pane windows, there are decorative cast-iron casement windows opening at the verandah level. Two symmetrical placed chimneys complete the picturesque appearance of the house. The 'Regency Cottage' in Wool was built along similar lines.

Although the idealised rural cottage became firmly established during the Regency period, the impetus towards the picturesque had started much earlier, in the eighteenth century. A few prosperous landowners in Dorset built groups of model cottages, often in pairs, landscaped into the surrounding scenery for the rural labourers working on their estates.

Perhaps the best known of these model estate villages lies at Milton Abbas. Capability Brown developed the whole village site, in a wooded valley, for Joseph Damer, including the creation of an artificial lake, during the period 1771-90. The now splendid-looking wide street of square white cob-walled cottages runs up the hill from the lake at the bottom. Wide grass verges border the road. When the identical pairs of thatched cottages were constructed in their straight neat rows, they were far from ideal for the occupants. Most lived in poverty and overcrowded conditions. Each rectangular cottage was designed for two families and there was only one room front and back on each floor. The central doorway led into a small vestibule, with lateral doorways opening into the two tenements on each side. Many of the cottage pairs have since been converted into single larger cottages.

Parts of the lovely village of Witchampton bear some similarities to Milton Abbas, by the fact that many inhabitants moved there into the New Town area when their original village at More Crichel was demolished in the second half of the eighteenth century to create a more spacious park around Crichel House. The new cottages were built with cob and thatch but few now survive. The present older part of the village has many cottages displaying timber framework, with brick in-filling, and the majority have thatched roofs. Several have origins in the seventeenth century.

The building of model estate cottages continued into the nineteenth and twentieth centuries. Beginning in 1870, the Guest family built

Timber-framed cottages, near the churchyard at Witchampton. Many are thatched with long straw, in contrast to the combed wheat reed used in more western parts of the county.

One of the three blocks of Victorian terraced cottages built by Charlotte Guest at Canford Magna in 1870.

'The Homestead' built as the village club by James Ismay at Iwerne Minster in 1921 to enable those who used it 'to pass through life a little more pleasantly'. It had a rifle range, dance hall, card room, billiards room, ladies parlour and tea room.

Thatched estate cottages at Bladen Valley, Briantspuddle, the creation of Sir Ernest Debenham, the founder of Debenham's stores.

model terraced cottages in mock-Tudor style at Canford Magna, complete with ornamented chimneys, lattice windows and gabled tiled roofs. The walls were constructed with buff and terracotta moulded bricks, locally made at Parkstone. The cottage interiors were more utilitarian, with tiny bedrooms and the front doors opened directly into the living rooms; rustic porches were later added between 1886 and 1896.

Another rich benefactor, James Ismay of Iwerne Minster, was associated with the brick and half-timbered cottages constructed in the village, an uncommon combination of building materials for Dorset. In 1921, James Ismay financed the building of the village club, known as 'The Homestead', which was furnished with a half-timbered porch, in keeping with the architectural style of the village. As well as his concern for the well-being of his workers, he introduced modern agricultural methods to both cereal growing and animal breeding.

Similar motives prompted Sir Ernest Debenham to build estate cottages at Bladen Valley, Briantspuddle, in the 1920s. Here the picturesque thatched cottages stand each side of a cul-de-sac, with the war memorial at the top. The cottages are arranged in various groups.

Part of 'The Ring' at Briantspuddle, built by Sir Ernest Debenham as a dairy; it has since been converted into a series of terraced cottages.

The roofs offer a variety of ornamented thatch designs; wide green verges run along the fronts of the cottages (two of which were tragically destroyed by fire in 2002).

Sir Ernest was also responsible for 'The Ring' at Briantspuddle. Although now converted to cottages, it was originally part of a model dairy complex. The two-storey building, with a one-storey centre block, was unusually constructed with locally made cavity concrete bricks, as an experiment to reduce interior condensation in the dairy. Two ornamental turrets were built at each end of the building and furnished with conical bonnets of thatch. Sir Ernest also had an influence on the provision of some excellent cottages in the nearby village of Milborne St Andrew, where he had established a large milk factory. The projects were aimed to encourage self-sufficiency and prevent the migration of workers to the towns. Like James Ismay in Iwerne Minster, Sir Ernest introduced the most modern farming methods, using the wealth amassed from his London drapery business to create a huge integrated farm providing hundreds of local jobs.

THE MEDIEVAL PERIOD

Several medieval farmhouses survive in Dorset, such as Barnston Farm at Church Knowle and Naish Farm at Holwell; both described earlier as examples of the open hall design of farmhouse, which became the characteristic medieval domestic plan. Another farmhouse of this type is Lodge Farm, which stands about a mile from Pamphill and was also once used as a hunting lodge. Formerly a part of the medieval Kingston Lacy estate, the building dates to the fifteenth century. It was constructed with stone rubble walls under a tiled and stone-slate roof, with a first floor great hall and solar, divided by an oak screen. The ground floor was probably used as a store, or possibly as a service room. The medieval windows were fashioned with two cusped arched lights. In general, medieval mullioned windows at the vernacular level

Lodge Farm at Pamphill. The stone slates are only found on the lower courses of the roof, where their heavy weight is supported by the wall structure. The rest of the roof is tiled.

The medieval Senior's Farm at Marnhull may originally have housed monks from Glastonbury Abbey, who once owned the parish.

were made in either stone or wood. They usually consisted of a horizontal range with a series of vertical lancet lights, or a series of diamond mullioned divisions in the window frame. Many medieval buildings, including manor houses that later became farmhouses originally incorporated a defensive element. One such medieval farmhouse, Godlingston Manor, has a stone-slate roof and a fortified defensive tower with five feet thick walls.

About half-a-mile north of Corscombe lies Corscombe Court. A moat formerly surrounded the L-shaped late thirteenth or early fourteenth-century farmhouse and its ancillary farm buildings, which include a fifteenth-century barn; all arranged around a square yard. The farmstead has suffered many later additions and alterations but still retains its basic medieval form. It was probably a former grange to Sherborne Abbey, when it nestled in a forest clearing.

Senior's Farm, built near the church at Marnhull, is thought to date from the end of the fifteenth century. Originally, it was probably built as a grange to Glastonbury Abbey, whose abbot was the Lord of the Manor. Stone rubble walls support a roof of tiles and stone-slates. An enlargement of the two-storey building took place in the eighteenth century, when a further wing was added. Another fifteenth-century farmhouse, Higher Farm, at Margaret Marsh, near Shaftesbury has a thatched roof sheltering the stone rubble walls. Originally an open hall

Top A sweeping two level thatched roof shelters Higher Farm at Margaret Marsh, another medieval survivor.

Above The blocked window near the centre of the long building once admitted light to the open hall of Upbury Farm at Yetminster, before the insertion of its upper floor.

design, the farmhouse was built with a two-storey service bay on one side of the hall and a further bay on the opposite side. Smoke from an open hearth escaped through a smoke-hole in the open hall roof. The hall was chambered over in the sixteenth century, when an upper floor was inserted and a chimney-stack constructed through the thatch. Part of the hall was then made into a through-passage. Several of the original roof timbers remain, including parts of an early wattle ceiling. Upbury Farm, at Yetminster, built in the fifteenth century with locally quarried stone was also originally an open hall house. Again the central open hall was chambered over in the late sixteenth century, making a two-storey farmhouse. Slates cover the roof, supported on collar-beam timbers and curved braces.

Church Farm, at Trent, was built in the late fourteenth or early fifteenth century and the two-storey building was constructed with a mixture of rubble and ashlar. The farmhouse once possessed a hall with two cross-wings but one wing has disappeared with the passage of time. The building has endured many alterations through the centuries and the roof is now covered with slates.

Turning to cottages, a late medieval one survives opposite 'The Ring' at Briantspuddle. The thatched 'Cruck Cottage' built of cob, in the late fifteenth century, has since been considerably reconstructed with stone rubble and has undergone many alterations and extensions. It was originally built with four cruck trusses under the thatch, to shelter an open hall of two bays, with a third bay for service rooms. Another thatched cottage, opposite the memorial seat and village green at Tolpuddle, preserves some partially exposed roof trusses that date to the fourteenth century.

'Cruck Cottage', Briantspuddle. Until recently, the ridge of the thatched roof would have been plain and not in the present ornamented block form.

Pitchmarket, Abbey Street, Cerne Abbas, a rare example of medieval timber-framed cottages still surviving in Dorset.

Timber-framed cottages were relatively rare in Dorset, so it is fortunate that a few have survived from the medieval period. The Pitchmarket row of cottages, on the west side of Abbey Street, Cerne Abbas, dates to around 1500; one of which was a former pub, 'The Nag's Head Inn'. They were constructed in two-storeys, with timber-framed stone walls under heavy stone-slate roofs. The exterior walls may once have been completely covered with plaster, thus preserving the timber hidden underneath. The jettied upper storeys of the cottages display elaborately moulded corbelling and some of the doorway jambs also possess medieval mouldings. At the time, jettied storeys were a status symbol in rural areas. The large windows would originally have been fitted with shutters, as glazing was unusual, even for quite superior houses. In most houses, glazing did not become common until the seventeenth century, when small 'bottle' glass windows came into use. In 1696 a window tax was introduced, causing a reduction in the number of widows. Only the mass-production of sheet glass from 1840 onwards meant that the humblest cottages could have glazed windows, especially after the repeal of the window tax in 1851.

TUDOR AND STUART

Dorset possesses a number of Tudor farmhouses and cottages. Although brick became the characteristic building material of the Tudor period and plaster was often used to simulate stone, the practice did not spread widely in Dorset. For the vernacular construction of farmhouses and cottages, stone rubble was more favoured. Many of the manor houses built in the period were later converted to farmhouses. One such Tudor timber-framed manor house nestles in the village of Hammoon (see frontispiece). The history of the manor farmhouse, built of stone ashlar and rubble under a thatched roof, makes an interesting study. The main body of the house was probably built around 1500 but the grand porch at the front has a shaped gable and strapwork. This impressive Purbeck limestone porch is probably

The late sixteenth-century plaster ceiling in the drawing room of Church Farm, Trent – an example of Tudor wealth improving a medieval farmhouse

A Tudor manor house, known as Little Toller Farm built by John Samways at Toller Fratrum. The tiny hamlet takes its name from the *fratrum*, or 'brothers', of the Knights of St John of Jerusalem, who once owned it.

of the Elizabethan or Jacobean period and therefore dates to about 1600, a century later than the main house. The L-shaped farmhouse has undergone many alterations and additions, from the seventeenth to the nineteenth century. Haydon Farm, at Lydlinch, is another L-shaped farmhouse of the same period but on a smaller scale. It was built with a through passage, with plank-and-muntin partitions.

Another Tudor manor house that became a farmhouse may be found at Toller Fratrum. John Samways, a Dorchester merchant purchased the hamlet in 1540. The grey stone two-storey house, known as Little Toller Farm, dates back to the mid-sixteenth century. The long narrow building displays two spectacular tall twisted chimneys on a central-gabled chimney-breast, which projects from the main tiled roof. Intriguingly, a carved gable finial of a chained monkey, holding a mirror, rises between the two chimneys. As well as the main house, John Samways was also responsible for the building of the long thatched single-storey stable block, with its Tudor windows, that lies at right angles to the main house. The outbuilding bears the family crest of the Samways.

Although the basic structure of West Cruxton Farmhouse at Maiden Newton is sixteenth century, the three-storey porch was added later.

At nearby Maiden Newton is West Cruxton Farm, a sixteenth-century farmhouse built with banded flint and stone under a thatched roof and an internal spiral staircase. Some of the original stone buttresses support the walls and a few of the original stone-mullioned windows also remain. Ham Hill stone-mullioned windows also survive in Sturt Farmhouse, at Stalbridge Weston; this three-bay fronted Tudor house was built with stone rubble under a tiled roof.

Moonfleet Farmhouse, also called Lower Farm, at Higher Ansty was built with stone rubble during the middle of the sixteenth century; it is likely that some of the material used was salvaged from nearby Milton Abbey after the Dissolution of the Monasteries. However, the thatched building has since undergone several extensions to create a substantial house, with a right-angled wing added to the original block. One of the main ground floor rooms boasts a rare Cyma-Cavetto ceiling structure, consisting of longitudinal and transverse interlocking carved beams. This represents one of the few surviving coffered ceilings of this type in England.

The village of Pimperne possibly conceals a former Elizabethan

Moonfleet Farmhouse at Higher Ansty. A sympathetic blending of many later additions to the basic sixteenth-century middle section.

farmhouse, now used as The Anvil restaurant. For many years, the property was thought most likely of eighteenth-century origin, built as four separate cob-walled cottages. However, during extensive restoration work carried out in 1958 when the cottages were combined, the original roof-line was disclosed and the property in its present integrated form is now thought to represent the original layout of the Elizabethan farmhouse. Osmington possesses Charity Farm, built as a long-house in the late sixteenth century. The original roof has disappeared and a galvanised iron one substituted. Dorset once had several so-called 'charity farms' that were purchased by donation from various benefactors. The rents obtained from leasing the farms were used to assist the poor and in the case of the Osmington farm, also to pay for an annual sermon.

'Pear Tree Cottage' at Piddletrenthide was built of banded flint and rubble under a thatched roof, with a through passage. Inside, an altar stone, probably salvaged from a demolished church after the Reformation was used as the lintel for one of the fireplaces. Another Tudor cottage stands in The Square at Puddletown; it was built in

The former home of the Dorset-born writer Ralph Wightman,
a Tudor cottage in The Square at Puddletown.

1573, according to a stone over one of the windows. It was constructed with banded flint and ashlar, again under a thatched roof, and fitted with three-light mullioned windows and hood-moulds. Ralph Wightman, the Dorset-born writer and broadcaster once lived in the cottage. An even older thatched cottage, built around 1525, is located in Spetisbury; Marigold Cottage is now used as a restaurant. Yetminster provides a good example of a Dorset village built with local limestone; old farms and cottages flank the main street and some date to the Tudor period.

Dorset claims a wealth of Stuart manor houses, later converted to farmhouses. Two such properties may be found at Trent and Fontmell Magna, both aptly named Manor Farm. A few farmhouses of the Stuart period were, unusually for Dorset, built with timber-framed walls. One example, Walnut Farm, lies on the Kingston Lacy estate; the two-storey building has a thatched roof. Another example is the seventeenth-century thatched farmhouse that stands beside God's Blessing Green, near Wimborne.

Several of the stone buildings in the village of Powerstock date back to the seventeenth century, including Wytherstone Farm. This was

Wytherstone Farm, Powerstock. A fireplace on the first floor bears the scratched initials and date 'W.T. 1615, E.T.'.

built as a two-storey farmhouse, with rubble walls under a slate roof. It has three chimneys, one at each gable end and one in the centre. The farmhouse retains some of its original fireplaces and one reveals the date, 1615. The barn near the house is even earlier, probably built in the sixteenth century. Centre arches of the collar-beam type, with curved timbers, support its thatched roof. Generally, Tudor and Stuart barns were not built in isolation but as part of the farmstead group, unlike some of their earlier medieval counterparts.

A rather rare sight, a Queen Anne thatched farmhouse, lies beside the road at Bovington, near Lawrence of Arabia's cottage at Cloud's Hill. The beautifully proportioned Bovington Farmhouse consists of

A central thatched porch located vertically in line below the two windows above maintains the symmetry of Bovington Farmhouse.

Gold Hill, Shaftesbury. Two of the cottages were built at the end of the seventeenth century, originally of thatch with rubble walls.

two storeys with an attic. It was built at the end of the Stuart period, in the early eighteenth century, with red brick on a rubble plinth, but many alterations have since been made.

Two contrasting seventeenth-century farmhouses may be found at Netherbury and Kingston. Woodcombe Farmhouse, at Netherbury, was built as a single-storey dwelling of the long-house type but a second floor was added in the eighteenth century; whilst Scoles Farm, near Kingston (for illustration see page 4), was built with Purbeck stone rubble and parts of a medieval hall house were incorporated into its structure.

St John's Farmhouse at Hinton Martell was built in the early seventeenth century but was later divided into two cottages. As well as farmhouse conversions, many individual Stuart period cottages survive in Dorset. A few of these border the cobbled lane that constitutes picturesque Gold Hill at Shaftesbury. They were built with stone rubble and most were roofed with tiles or stone-slates. Two were later modified and heightened to accommodate thatched roofs. Two

The two adjacent cottages at Wakeham before their conversion into Portland Museum.

thatched cottages on Portland, built of stone in 1640, were later renovated and converted into the local museum by public subscription, after being donated to the island by Dr Marie Stopes, the pioneer of birth control and a long time resident. One of the cottages, known as Avice's, was where the heroine lived in Thomas Hardy's novel, *The Well-Beloved*.

Abbotsbury delights the eye with its golden limestone cottages, built with stone obtained from the former quarries at Portesham. Several of the cottages date to the seventeenth century and again many are roofed with thatch, harvested from the local reed beds. Another stone built village is Church Knowle, but here the cottages were constructed with local Purbeck stone. 'The Old Cottage' in the village is seventeenth century, the same age as the nearby 'New Inn'. The village of Kimmeridge also possesses some Stuart stone-walled cottages; likewise, Litton Cheney has several strung along its winding streets. Most are thatched and built with rubble. Shapwick has some cottages by the church, built originally with cob walls, several of

Opposite page top 'Court Cottage' on Cowgrove Common lies west of the Court House. The thatched timber-framed cottage dates to the seventeenth century and still retains its original overhang or verandah with an earthen floor.

Opposite page below 'Hangman's Cottage', Dorchester, is located on a well-known site by the River Frome.

which were clad with brick in 1727 to strengthen the cob structure.

Cowgrove Common, near Pamphill, has 'Court Cottage' (until recently 'Lower Dairy Cottage'), with an unusual thatched verandah. It is thought that the cottage may be a modification of a single-storey open hall house, with a central fireplace, the smoke from which would have escaped through a hole in the roof. Pamphill also preserves several other seventeenth-century cottages, some of which have timber-framed walls.

Finally, a thatched cottage built in the early seventeenth century, on the northern outskirts of Dorchester, later became the home of the town executioner. At that time, the gallows stood near the present junction of Icen Way and South Walks in Dorchester. The last public executions held in Dorchester were in 1863. 'Hangman's Cottage', situated by the water meadows, has since been extended and modernized, to create a long attractive dwelling much photographed by visitors.

THE GEORGIAN PERIOD

Georgian terraced town houses are usually three storeys high, with their first floor multi-pane windows set within high recessed arches. Their balanced sash windows came into universal use during the eighteenth century. In contrast, Georgian vernacular buildings exhibit a wide variety of simpler forms – although most of those built for the poor have long since disappeared, leaving only those that were more solidly built. Many Georgian manor farmhouses in Dorset have two storeys and mullioned windows.

The disastrous fires that swept through many Dorset towns during the eighteenth century demanded the rebuilding of houses and cottages. As a result, Dorset has inherited a remarkable legacy of fine Georgian architecture. Blandford Forum presents the most outstanding example, as an entire new town centre arose out of the ashes, after the tragic fire of 1731. Another fire, in 1762, destroyed much of Wareham, including public buildings and 133 dwellings. The

A plain terrace of Georgian cottages, with gabled attic windows and period sash windows at Bere Regis.

Georgian cottages in Market Street in the Old Town area of Poole.

rebuilding resulted in many late eighteenth-century houses and cottages, of which several semi-detached cottages were constructed with brick. As a consequence of the fire, the use of thatch as a roofing material, the main cause of the disaster, was banned.

Despite this, thatch still remained the usual roofing material in most villages during the Georgian period, except in Purbeck where stone-slates were used. Most cottages continued to be built one room deep. The use of thatch also caused several villages to be destroyed by fire during the seventeenth and eighteenth centuries. Bere Regis was just one to suffer badly and, after the fire of 1788, terraces of new Georgian cottages were erected in place of those destroyed. Fire was not the sole ravager of villages. Man also played a role. The best example was probably the deliberate destruction of Milton Abbas, before its re-creation as Dorset's most famous Georgian village.

Even in the twentieth century, wholesale devastation of old dwellings has continued. For example, the Old Town in Poole underwent a planned demolition of nearly a thousand properties in the 1950s and 1960s, to allow redevelopment. Many of its Georgian cottages were thought too expensive to renovate. Fortunately, a small area around Market Street, in the Old Town, has since been conserved and retains several delightful Georgian cottages.

A delightful collection of Georgian thatched cottages at Tarrant Monkton.

Further north, Tarrant Monkton has many eighteenth-century cob-walled cottages bordering both sides of the stream that meanders through it. Okeford Fitzpaine has many cottages of the same date built, in an unusual combination for Dorset, of brick with some timber framing. Some walls have alternating bands of brick and flint. Sydling St Nicholas has several Georgian cottages constructed with banded stone and flint. Hinton St Mary used stone for the construction of its eighteenth-century dwellings. Likewise, stone obtained from the quarry at Winspit formed the building material for the eighteenth-century cottages at Worth Matravers. At Corfe Castle, the local Purbeck stone was used for both walls and roofs. Unusually, a couple of cottages in East Street have brick porches.

Charmouth contains a few stone walled cottages built in the seventeenth century and also preserves many good Georgian and Regency examples, some with bow windows. Similarly, Shapwick, as well as seventeenth-century cottages, shelters some Georgian ones by the church. Lyme Regis is a late Georgian resort and again many cottages possess bow or bay windows.

A tiny secluded cottage built for a gamekeeper or woodsman in about 1808 is one of the best-known Georgian cottages in Dorset. It lies on the heath, about a mile north of Bovington Army Camp and is now cared for by The National Trust. It is T.E. Lawrence's (of Arabia) former home at Cloud's Hill. Lawrence purchased the cottage, made of brick with a tiled roof, in 1925. The tiny interior of the dwelling remains virtually untouched, and is as it was when he lived in it. It contains his furniture, personal belongings and other relics. There are two upper rooms, one of which is minuscule and two downstairs rooms. The entrance door of the cottage is set in a windowless wall. The philosophic Greek inscription over the door broadly translates into 'Does not care', or 'Why worry'. The thatched outbuilding beside the cottage is almost certainly where Lawrence garaged his Brough Superior motorcycle, before his untimely death on it in a road accident in 1935.

An even more famous cottage, the birthplace of Thomas Hardy in 1840, nestles on the edge of Puddletown heath. Thomas Hardy's great-grandfather built the thatched two-storey cottage at Higher Bockhampton in 1800. The National Trust acquired it in 1947. The walls were constructed with cob but without deep dug foundations, as

A former gamekeeper's cottage at Bovington, and named Cloud's Hill in Victorian times. In the twentieth century it became the home of T.E. Lawrence (of Arabia) after he joined the Tank Corps.

The cottage at Higher Bockhampton in which Thomas Hardy was born in 1840, and wrote *Under the Greenwood Tree* and *Far from the Madding Crowd,* is the most famous and frequently visited cottage in Dorset.

was once the usual practice. A facing of bricks was added to protect the cob, making the walls about two feet thick. The use of this technique suggested that the owner, Hardy's great-grandfather, could afford a better quality cottage than most. In fact, he was a stone mason who also occasionally indulged in a little brandy smuggling: he could watch for the approach of an excise man by peering through a squint he incorporated in the porch. The interior of the cottage was made fairly spacious and the kitchen was furnished with a traditional inglenook fireplace and bread oven. Thomas Hardy was born in the middle bedroom of the three upstairs rooms and later wrote his first five books there.

Although most cottages were relatively small, there were a much greater variety of sizes in farmhouses. Upper Farm at Lillington represents a typical eighteenth-century farmstead with a dairy, cider house, cottage and cow-shed clustering around the main farmhouse. Early Georgian farmhouses were usually of this type, being sited within the farmstead. However, as mentioned earlier, a notable feature

Just outside Dorchester, near Came, lies Herringston Dairy House. The use of brick for the building of farmhouses in Dorset became common during the eighteenth and nineteenth centuries, although here it was only used in the upper storey.

of the later Georgian period was the building of larger farmhouses away from the actual farm. Lower Farm, at Stoke Abbot, represents a typical L-shape two-storey farmhouse. It was built with stone ashlar in 1748 and unusually fitted with stone mullion windows. The fashion of incorporating such windows in Georgian buildings had generally ceased earlier in the century. An example of a late Georgian/Regency farmhouse stands on the minor road linking Herringston with Came, just outside Dorchester. Herringston Dairy House consists of a long two-storey building, constructed with brick for the upper storey and rubble for the lower. Two chimney-stacks protrude through its hipped thatched roof.

THE VICTORIANS

The growing industrialization of the nineteenth century slowly brought changes to Dorset's farms. The majority of farm buildings altered little in design during Victoria's reign but were adapted in minor ways to cope with new technology and to improve the farmers' living accommodation. Only the wealthier farmers could initially afford mechanization, such as the use of steam engines to power the threshing machines introduced in the 1830s. In many cases, horses continued to be used to drive farm machinery until the end of the nineteenth century.

Although only a small number of new farmhouses were built during the period, due to the general amalgamation of farms, those that were possessed more rooms than their Georgian counterparts and their roofs were generally slated. Any new building work carried out was done in the prosperous mid-Victorian years, before the agricultural depression gathered pace in the late 1870s. Dairy farmers fared the best during the depression. If a cottage was built it was usually to

Bridge Farmhouse, at Hooke is a good example of a late Victorian farmhouse set in the centre of its dairy farm.

Local stone built cottages in Hope Terrace, Martinstown.

accommodate a married son, sharing the farm with his father. Alternatively, when a farm was large enough, two sons who inherited sometimes decided to divide the land, so that each could farm independently. Again, this necessitated the building of another cottage.

Rich landowners continued to build tied cottages for their workers, to retain their labour and discourage migration to the towns. Some farmhouses left redundant by the amalgamation of two or more farms were converted into cottages for labourers. Any new cottages were usually built in the vernacular tradition that survived much longer in Dorset than in many other parts of the country. For example, in the mid-nineteenth century, many buildings at Martinstown were built with stone obtained from the Upwey quarry and at Powerstock, cottages were built with local materials. Bridge Farmhouse, at Hooke, was constructed in 1898 with stone obtained from Marnhull. However, in most areas, the end of the nineteenth century marked the end of any substantial vernacular content in new cottages and farmhouses. By this time, the railways had become well-established and mass produced products, such as slates, bricks and tiles, could be moved around the country with relative ease. The end of the century also saw the introduction of concrete for the foundations of farm buildings and cottages.

The living conditions of farm labourers in Dorset varied considerably during the nineteenth century, those in the west faring worst. In Powerstock, for example, some cottagers lived with ground floors of trampled earth and climbed by ladder to an upper floor under the rafters. As mentioned earlier, most cottages were still grossly overcrowded.

The plight of the urban poor was little better, specially once closely packed terraced cottages were constructed in the second half of the nineteenth century. The solitary room at ground level opened directly onto the street. Upstairs there was one, or at the most two rooms. The cottages contained no lavatory, larder or coal house. Overcrowding and inadequate sanitation brought disease and outbreaks of cholera. Even the county town, Dorchester, retained cesspool drainage throughout the whole of the nineteenth century.

Outside privies at country cottages and farmhouses presented less of a health problem because they were relatively few in number and were well-spaced apart. Four separate rows of terraced cottages with improved sanitation were built in Puddletown during the period 1864 to 1870. They were the inspiration of John Brymer, who lived in the nearby Ilsington House, after purchasing the estate from the Earl of Orford. The dates and initials of the benefactor were proudly carved in stone shields on the terraces. The Square at Puddletown also retains a row of early nineteenth-century thatched cottages, with upper bow windows.

Victorian cottages built by Lord Alington on the Crichel Estate provided much-improved living conditions for the local estate workers.

Above As well as terraced cottages, John Brymer also built in Puddletown this stone walled cottage bearing his crest, placed centrally below the eaves.

Below Thatched cottages at The Square, Puddletown, in 1891. Pillars support the attractive oriel window of the left-hand cottage, which remains largely unchanged today.

Victorian seaside cottages on Marine Parade, Lyme Regis, with tall imposing semi-circular bow-windows.

Rows of late Victorian terraced cottages are now a familiar sight in most Dorset towns and villages. When constructed, each terrace was designed as an individual long building to give an overall pleasing architectural view. However, householders have since imposed their own individualities on them. Some have replaced Welsh slates with tiles; others have inserted modern double glazed windows in place of the original wooden sash ones. Others have stone cladding shielding their brick walls, and the cottages are often painted different colours. The resulting hotchpotch presents an appearance far removed from the original conception of the architect.

Lyme Regis, although noted for its Georgian and Regency cottages, also has the delightful two-storey thatched terrace of Madeira Cottages, built around 1840 in Marine Parade. The cottages, with bow windows, were originally designed for rich Victorians to spend their holidays directly on the sea front. The design represented an extension of the desire for the picturesque, nurtured on a more lavish scale during the earlier cottage *ornée* period.

Similarly, as mentioned earlier, the village of Canford Magna offers a Victorian version of model estate cottages, built with ornamented brick. As well as the Victorians' love of restoring churches and building highly ornamented edifices, they also, on the vernacular scale, designed windows for cottages that were appreciably taller than the square ones used in earlier periods. These gave better ventilation and some of the better class cottages possessed moulded frames around the windows.

As in earlier times, fire remained a permanent threat. A spark from a wheelwright's workshop started a fire that swiftly spread and destroyed nearly all of Sixpenny Handley in 1892, leaving one hundred homeless and causing the majority of the village to be rebuilt. By contrast, Kimmeridge has a row of cottages built in the middle of the nineteenth century for miners who never occupied them. The plan to convert the local bituminous shale deposits into a solid fuel was impractical, due to the high sulphur content giving rise to a foul odour, and the company failed before the bulk of the workforce took up residence.

Several tollhouses, built in Dorset to control the turnpike roads, have since been converted into homes. One example is the 'Old Turnpike Cottage', at Tarrant Hinton, built around 1840 with rendered walls and a slate roof. As well as tollhouses, many nineteenth-century lodges that guarded the entrances to large estates have since been converted to private residences.

Finally, mention must be made of Bournemouth, a town that did not exist two hundred years ago. It is therefore wholly Victorian in origin. At the beginning of the nineteenth century it was a deserted

'Cliff Cottage', photographed here in 1863, was one of the earliest houses built at Bourne Mouth, dating to about 1812.

A picturesque cottage at Talbot village, Talbot Woods. The village was named after the wealthy Talbot sisters, Georgina Charlotte and Marianne, who owned a large estate in the area.

heath by the mouth of the River Bourne, until wealthy gentlemen such as Lewis Tregonwell, started to build a few isolated holiday cottages there. Parts of Tregonwell's later mansion still survive, having been incorporated into the Royal Exeter Hotel: unfortunately, none of the original cottages remain. Gradually, a whole marine village developed and by the middle of the nineteenth century Bournemouth's popularity was assured. In the 1860s the two unmarried daughters of Sir George Talbot financed the building of an almshouse and several cottages in Talbot Woods, on the west side of Bournemouth. The Portland stone almshouse was built to alleviate the conditions under which the elderly formerly lived on the nearby barren heath. By the end of the nineteenth century, Bournemouth had grown to a fashionable resort with a population of nearly 60,000.

THE TWENTIETH CENTURY

The dawn of the twentieth century heralded an improvement in the quality of houses and cottages. The use of mass-produced bricks and slates became widespread and properties became subject to building regulations. Although bricks, slates and the use of concrete became common, the local traditional style was still kept alive in some areas, such as Sir Ernest Debenham's picturesque development at Briantspuddle in 1919. A little later, in 1934, Sir Raymond Unwin, designed the six T.U.C. Memorial Cottages on the western fringe of Tolpuddle, in honour of its martyrs transported to Australia in 1834.

Thompson Dagnell's recently erected stone sculpture of the leader of the Tolpuddle Martyrs, George Loveless, stands in front of the T. U. C. Memorial Cottages at Tolpuddle.

Each cottage bears the name of one of the six men; James Loveless, George Loveless, Thomas Stanfield, John Stanfield, James Hammet and James Brine. Elsewhere, the 1930s brought the widespread building of semi-detached houses throughout the county.

The concept of council or social housing in England was first envisaged in 1898 to take over the limited role formerly played by the charities. The building of council houses gradually progressed through the twentieth century and increased markedly immediately after the two World Wars. In particular, the end of the Second World War saw a huge increase in the rate of council house building. It also saw the introduction of the prefab to help alleviate the housing shortage. Although initially intended for use as small temporary homes, some prefabs in Dorset became permanent residences well into the second half of the twentieth century. The building of council housing also took place in villages, as well as in towns. At the end of the millennium, West Dorset alone had about five thousand such properties. In the last two decades of the century, some council houses were sold to their tenants, while others were transferred to the care of housing associations.

'Midway Cottage', sympathetically built in 2000 in the local vernacular style at Grange, Furzehill, near Wimborne.

New cottages built in Redlands Lane, Broadwindsor, using traditional local materials.

The private development of houses and cottages has also continued. For instance, Charminster has grown considerably and likewise Puddletown has undergone housing expansion on its western and southern fringes. The villages of Allington and Bradpole have been nearly absorbed or overshadowed by the spread of their larger neighbour Bridport. Whilst in the east, Holdenhurst still retains its village green but urban sprawl threatens to engulf its surrounding countryside.

In the last decade of the twentieth century, about two thousand new homes were annually built in the Dorset countryside. Dorset County Council estimates that this rate would probably continue until 2016. This is despite the fact that 53 percent of the county is designated an Area of Outstanding Natural Beauty, compared to the 15 percent average for the rest of England.

Many villages have become victims of a creeping suburbia and are losing their original vernacular character, with the new cottages and houses often surrounding the older ones that nestle around the church. Sometimes even old cottages have been demolished to make room for new ones. Outward expansion has devoured huge areas of former

A development at West Mead, Bridport, includes an assortment of new houses built at the turn of the twenty-first century.

open countryside. Sometimes, the changes are so subtle that residents do not notice or care, unless a large housing estate is proposed next door to them. The majority of people now living in the villages and hamlets are no longer connected with farming, despite the fact that they are surrounded by farmland. Many have retired to live in the country and others commute to work in the towns. Fortunately, Dorset's planners have now become more sensitive to local architectural styles and builders are being encouraged to blend their architecture with that of neighbouring old properties. The few builders who specialize in this field have to strike a balance between cost and accurate replication of the traditional vernacular style. Several cottages have been built with the exteriors displaying the local character, while the interiors offer all the modern conveniences demanded for twenty-first century living.

St Catherine's Terrace, Abbotsbury, was constructed using the building traditions of West Dorset to harmonise with the rest of the village.

At Abbotsbury, small new clusters of cottages have been created conforming to the local building traditions of West Dorset. The walls are built with flint, brick and ashlar banding, with the roofs topped with thatch. West Mead on the western fringe of Bridport, along the main road towards Symondsbury, enjoys a similar type development of 27 properties. The cottage walls are again constructed with flint and brick, with some flint banding. Some of the cottages are roofed with thatch and others with recycled clay tiles and slates. The new cottages again follow the local building tradition, except of course for the presence of some integral garages, highlighting a blending of a modern essential with the old. A similar building programme of semi-detached cottages has taken place at Winterbourne Whitechurch. Higher Bockhampton also has some new traditional style cottages, with flint and stone-banded walls under thatched roofs. Likewise, Broadwindsor and Burton Bradstock contain new cottages that harmonize with the local architecture. Further cottage homes, with a traditional look, have recently been built, on the outskirts of Blandford Forum and at Hazelbury Bryan; the latter having sweeping views of the Blackmore Vale.

POUNDBURY

The Prince of Wales has carried forward, on a large scale, the concept of building cottages whose exteriors display a mixture of Dorset's traditional styles. Instead of isolated groups of cottages, a whole village is in the process of being created at Middle Farm, on Duchy of Cornwall land at Poundbury, to the west of Dorchester. The site is situated on high ground, in contrast to most Dorset towns and villages, which have historically grown along valleys. Leon Krier, a specialist in urban design, prepared the overall blueprint for the project and the building of the first stage commenced in 1993, with the planned construction of 244 cottages and flats. This stage of the project was completed in 2001. The cottages incorporate all the requirements of twenty-first century living, such as double glazing, modern bathrooms and kitchens, high-efficiency boilers and water meters, despite their 'olde-worlde' look when viewed from the outside.

The types of cottages and houses cover a range of Dorset traditional architectural styles, from the fifteenth to the nineteenth centuries. Most properties have their fronts facing directly on the street, with their gardens at the rear. Several possess arcades and most have sash windows and chimneys. Some mid-eighteenth-century style town houses are included, with their front elevations scaled down in size from the original Georgian ones they emulate. They contrast with the brick and flint cottages, built in the Victorian style.

A large variety of building materials make up the construction of the cottages and houses. The wall materials include bricks, a few of which are laid in imitation Flemish Bond, to give the appearance of headers and stretchers being laid in the same course. Some walls are built with local stone used in various forms, including some stone cladding and rendering. A few properties are constructed with rough stones arranged in random courses, while others are built with smooth

A line of terraced cottages at Poundbury: random stone with Victorian sash windows.

dressed ashlar. Roofs consist of slates and tiles, with a lack of thatch, the most traditional of all Dorset's vernacular roofing materials. The many houses and cottages in close proximity would present a fire hazard if thatched and therefore infringe modern Building Regulations. Although in recent years Dorset local planners have agreed, with special provisions, the building of new thatched properties closer to their boundaries than previously allowed.

The most controversial part of the scheme has been the erection of the Fleur-de-Lis retirement apartments. The tall five-storey colossus

Opposite page Examples of the many different local architectural styles found on The Prince of Wales's development at Poundbury.
Left Random stone with Victorian sash windows.
Right Alternating wall banding with gable end and window surrounds in brick. *Bottom* Brick built with casement and bay windows.

that has arisen possesses twin-towers and dominates the other cottages, houses and public buildings. Although the siting of homes close to a prominent building is not unusual, many local residents ponder why a structure completely alien to Dorset's traditional architecture was selected.

Each district was planned so that its residents could both work and find recreational facilities within walking distance of their homes. To achieve this aim, light industrial factories, offices, shops, a pub, a restaurant and a market hall have been constructed. The hall has massive Bath stone columns, finished with Doric capitals, supporting the sharply pitched roof over the open ground floor and is the new home to a regular farmers' market selling local produce. As well as houses and public buildings, a main square and a series of smaller ones have been incorporated into the scheme, with pedestrian priority given over cars. In addition to privately owned cottages and houses, about 20 percent social housing has been included for renting to local people through the Guinness Trust.

Further developments on the adjoining land are envisaged, with building work lasting possibly until the 2020s, by which time 2,500 houses will have been built. The work will progress to a total of four districts and the complete development will eventually swallow up four hundred acres of Dorset's open green countryside; 250 of these being used for high-density housing and the remaining 150 for landscaping. The expansion will slowly spread westwards to the fringe of the Dorchester by-pass and increase the county town's population by approximately 5,000.

The Prince of Wales's determination to graft what is almost a rural village onto an existing town brings this book to a fitting conclusion. Even in the twenty-first century, the traditional architecture of Dorset's farmhouses and cottages has a part to play in shaping the future character of the county.

FURTHER READING

Bettey, J.H., *Man & The land - Farming in Dorset, 1846-1996*, 1996
Billett, M., *Thatched Buildings of Dorset*, 1984
Brown, R., *English Farmhouses*, 1982
Brown, R., *Timber-Framed Buildings of England*, 1986
Brunskill, R., *Vernacular Architecture*, 1971
Burnett, D., *Dorset: The County in Colour*, 1991
Clark, P., *Lady Wimborne Cottages*, 2000
Cook, O., *English Cottages and Farmhouses*, 1982
Cunnington, P., *How Old is Your House*, 1980
Draper, J., *Discover Dorset: The Georgians*, 1998
Draper, J., *Dorset: The Complete Guide*, 1984
Frith, F., *Dorset*, 1999
Gant, R., *Dorset Villages*, 1980
Hadfield, J. (editor), *The Shell Guide to England*, 1970
HMSO, *Historical Monuments in the County of Dorset* (8 volumes)
James, J., *Discover Dorset: The Victorians*, 1998
Kerr, B., *Bound to the Soil – A Social History of Dorset*, 1968
Legg, R., *National Trust Dorset*, 1987
Newman, J. and Pevsner, N., *Dorset: The Buildings of England*, 1972
Quiney, A., *The Traditional Buildings of England*, 1990
Taylor, C., *The Making of the English Landscape: Dorset*, 1970
Wightman, R., *Portrait of Dorset*, 1977
Wright, G., *The Stone Villages of Britain*, 1985

ACKNOWLEDGEMENTS

I would like to thank the following for allowing the inclusion of illustrations in their possession or for which they hold the copyright: Dorset County Museum; pages 8 and 63 (bottom): the Dovecote Press; back cover, pages 4, 9, 13, 14, 15, 17, 18, 23, 24, 26, 27, 28 (both), 29, 30, 31 (bottom), 32, 33, 35, 36 (both), 37, 38, 39, 40, 41 (both), 42, 43, 45, 48, 50, 51, 52 (both), 55, 57, 58, 61, 62, 63 (top), 54, 65, 66, 67, 68, 69, 71, 73, 75 (all): Royal Commission Historical Monuments (England); 10, 11, 20, 21, 34, 44, 46, 49 (top). The remaining photographs are from the author's collection. Christopher Chaplin drew the map on page 6 and the plans on pages 19 and 20. I am grateful to the Trustees of the Dorset County Museum for permission to use a detail from the watercolour of *Pigeon House Cottages* by H.J. Moule on the front cover.

INDEX

The

DISCOVER DORSET

Series of Books

A series of paperback books providing informative illustrated introductions to Dorset's history, culture and way of life. The following titles have so far been published.

BRIDGES *David McFetrich and Jo Parsons*
CASTLES AND FORTS *Colin Pomeroy*
CRANBORNE CHASE *Desmond Hawkins*
DRESS AND TEXTILES *Rachel Worth*
FARMHOUSES AND COTTAGES *Michael Billett*
FARMING *J.H.Bettey* FOLLIES *Jonathan Holt*
FOSSILS *Richard Edmonds* GEOLOGY *Paul Ensom*
THE GEORGIANS *Jo Draper*
THE INDUSTRIAL PAST *Peter Stanier*
ISLE OF PURBECK *Paul Hyland*
LEGENDS *Jeremy Harte* LOST VILLAGES *Linda Viner*
MILLS *Peter Stanier* PORTLAND *Stuart Morris*
POTTERY *Penny Copland-Griffiths*
THE PREHISTORIC AGE *Bill Putnam*
RAILWAY STATIONS *Mike Oakley*
REGENCY, RIOT AND REFORM *Jo Draper*
THE ROMANS *Bill Putnam*
SAXONS AND VIKINGS *David Hinton*
SHIPWRECKS *Maureen Attwooll*
STONE QUARRYING *Jo Thomas*
THE VICTORIANS *Jude James*

All the books about Dorset published by The Dovecote Press are available in bookshops throughout the county, or in case of difficulty direct from the publishers.
The Dovecote Press Ltd, Stanbridge,
Wimborne, Dorset BH21 4JD
Tel: 01258 840549 www.dovecotepress.com